AF408860

project management for ux design mastery

Navigating Project Management

william webb

Copyright © 2023 by William Webb

All rights reserved.

No part of this book may be reproduced in any form or by any electronic or mechanical means, including information storage and retrieval systems, without written permission from the author, except for the use of brief quotations in a book review.

contents

introduction

book overview

You've made a choice that will add depth and breadth to your UX design skills by picking up this book. Let's talk about what you can expect from the journey ahead and how you can make the most of it.

This book is designed to be your ultimate companion in understanding and applying project management principles to UX design, with an emphasis on the Scrum framework. We start by establishing solid foundations in UX design and project management, before venturing into the realm of Agile methodologies and Scrum, showing you how to intertwine these with your UX practice.

In the chapters that unfold, you'll find a mix of theory, case studies, practical examples, and tips. Each chapter is designed to build on the last, to gradually enhance your knowledge and understanding. You'll find plenty of real-world scenarios that demonstrate how these principles are applied in practice, and equip you with actionable insights you can take into your everyday work.

Chapter One and Two ensure we're all on the same page with understanding UX design and project management. If you're already a UX expert, you might skim these sections or use them for a quick refresher. Project management novices, on the other hand, will find these chapters a crucial resource to get a grasp on key concepts.

Chapter Three delves into the diverse tools and techniques in the project management world, introducing you to both traditional and Agile tools that can streamline your workflow and enhance productivity. We'll navigate the digital tools landscape together, discussing their pros, cons, and ideal scenarios for use.

Chapter Four and Five are where we dive deep into the Agile sea, with a keen focus on Scrum. Here, you'll understand what Scrum is, its various elements, and how it fits into the UX design sphere. You'll learn about its potential benefits and challenges, and how to effectively implement it in your UX projects.

Chapter Six takes you further into advanced Scrum practices for UX design. You'll learn how to incorporate user testing in Scrum sprints and how to maintain a user-centric focus amidst the quick turnaround times Scrum often demands.

Chapter Seven and Eight are dedicated to your role as a UX designer in project management, exploring how to navigate team dynamics, communicate with stakeholders, manage time and resources, and prioritize tasks and user needs effectively.

Finally, in Chapter Nine, we'll look to the horizon, discussing emerging trends and future skills needed in UX design and project management.

Now, how can you make the best use of this book? Remember, it's designed to be a flexible resource. Feel free to skip around if a particular topic catches your eye or if you're looking for information to solve a specific problem. There's no single right way to go about it - the path you take through the material is entirely up to you!

Practical examples and exercises peppered throughout the chapters serve to reinforce your learning. Whenever you encounter these, it's a good idea to pause and try them out. Get your hands dirty, that's where the real learning happens. This is a safe space to experiment, to make mistakes, and learn from them.

Lastly, don't forget to take advantage of the three appendices. The glossary will be an invaluable resource to you, the recommended reading and resources will help you take your learning further, and the templates and checklists will make your life as a UX designer dealing with project management a lot easier.

In essence, this book is your key to unlocking the synergies between UX design and project management. So, as you embark on this journey, remember that this isn't just a book—it's a map, a guide, and a toolbox, all rolled into one. Feel free to explore, dig deep, and put these lessons into action.

1 /
understanding ux design

the role of ux design in today's digital landscape

AS WE SET sail into the depths of the digital landscape, it's essential to understand the indispensable role UX design plays in navigating these waters. This chapter aims to illuminate the importance of UX design and its profound impact on the contemporary digital world.

User Experience, or UX, is not just a buzzword. It's the backbone of the digital world, shaping every interaction users have with websites, apps, and software. If we liken a digital product to an iceberg, what users see and interact with—the user interface (UI)—is merely the tip. Below the surface lies the vast expanse of UX design: the research, the user testing, the iterative design process, all aiming to create a seamless and enjoyable experience for the user.

In an era defined by technology and interconnectivity, the digital landscape is expanding and evolving at an unprecedented rate. Devices are smarter, apps are more sophisticated, and users are more digitally savvy than ever. People are no longer content with just 'functional'. They expect—and indeed, deserve—'exceptional'. This is where UX design steps in. It is the art and science of making digital experiences not just usable, but delightful.

In the early stages of the digital revolution, the focus was primarily on making things work. As long as a website loaded or an app didn't crash, it was deemed a success. But as technology evolved and competition heated up, merely 'working' was no longer good enough. A digital product had to stand out, to captivate users, to solve their problems in the simplest, most intuitive way possible. That's the essence of UX design —it's about empathy, about stepping into the user's shoes and seeing the digital world from their perspective.

To fully comprehend the magnitude of UX design's role, consider for a moment your favorite digital product—a website, an app, or a platform. Think about why you like it. Is it because it's aesthetically pleasing? Or because it's easy to navigate? Maybe it makes a complex task simple, or it just 'feels right' somehow. That 'right feeling' you're experiencing is no accident. It's the result of meticulous UX design, of understanding user needs and crafting an experience that meets those needs while providing delight.

UX design is now a crucial consideration for any business seeking to establish a robust digital presence. It's no longer a 'nice-to-have' but a 'must-have'. The reason is simple: good UX design translates to happier users, and happier users lead to higher engagement, increased customer loyalty, and ultimately, business success. In a market overflowing with choices, a well-designed user experience can be the competitive edge that sets a product apart.

The pervasiveness of UX design in today's digital landscape goes beyond just websites and apps. It's shaping the future of technology, driving innovation in fields like virtual reality, augmented reality, voice interface design, and beyond. As new technologies emerge and evolve, UX design will continue to play a pivotal role in shaping how these technologies are adopted and used, making them accessible, user-friendly, and enjoyable.

Now, you may wonder, "What does this mean for

me, as a UX designer?" Well, it means that you're not just a designer—you're an architect of the digital landscape. Your work has the power to shape experiences, influence perceptions, and change behaviors. It's an enormous responsibility, yes, but also an incredible opportunity. The digital world is your canvas, and with the brush of UX design in your hands, you can paint experiences that are not just functional and beautiful, but also meaningful and impactful.

In the chapters ahead, we'll delve deeper into the nuts and bolts of UX design and project management, providing you with the tools and techniques you need to master this craft. But for now, let's take a moment to appreciate the importance of the journey you're embarking on. UX design isn't just a job; it's a calling. It's about making the digital world a better, more inclusive, and delightful place for everyone.

the ux design process: an overview

Now that we've charted the vast influence of UX design in the digital landscape, it's time to unpack the magic behind it: the UX design process. This chapter is your treasure map to the process, illuminating each step in the journey from initial idea to final product. Let's embark on this exciting voyage of discovery!

To start, let's clarify what we mean by 'UX design process.' It is a methodology, a set of steps that UX designers follow to create a product that meets user needs and provides a delightful user experience. It's important to remember that while the process may seem linear on paper, in practice, it's more of a cycle—iterative and dynamic. Each project, each product, might necessitate variations or deviations from the process, but the fundamental principles remain the same.

The UX design process can be divided into five key stages: Research, Design, Prototype, Test, and Implement. Let's explore each stage and understand its significance.

1. Research: This is the foundation of the entire UX design process. It's about understanding the user and their needs, the market, and the business goals. Methods include user interviews, surveys, observations, competitive analysis, and more. The goal is to gather as much information as possible to make informed design decisions. It's crucial to approach this stage with an open mind—be ready to challenge assumptions and embrace surprises.

2. Design: With the insights from the research stage in hand, it's time to start designing. This involves creating user personas, user flow diagrams, and infor-

mation architecture. Then, you'll sketch, wireframe, and build mockups of your design. Throughout this stage, always refer back to your research and ensure your designs align with the user needs and business goals identified earlier.

3. Prototype: Here, the design comes to life. A prototype is a functional model of the design that lets users interact with it. It could be a low-fidelity prototype, like a paper sketch, or a high-fidelity one that closely mimics the final product. The idea is to provide a tangible representation of your design that goes beyond static images.

4. Test: Testing is where you validate your design decisions with real users. It involves observing users interacting with your prototype and gathering feedback. Methods can range from formal usability testing sessions to more casual user feedback rounds. It's critical to approach this stage with no preconceived notions—be ready to learn, adapt, and improve.

5. Implement: The final stage of the UX design process is implementation, where the validated design is developed into a final product. As a UX designer, your job doesn't end when you hand over the design to developers. You'll need to collaborate with them to ensure your design vision is accurately reflected in the final product.

That, in a nutshell, is the UX design process. Each

stage plays a critical role in shaping the final product, and the process's iterative nature allows for continuous learning and improvement. But remember, while the process provides a robust framework, it is not a strict recipe that must be followed verbatim. Each project may require different emphasis on different stages, or perhaps even an entirely different approach. The key lies in understanding the principles and adapting them to suit the task at hand.

core principles of ux design

We've now journeyed through the digital landscape and unpacked the UX design process. It's time to delve deeper into the very heart of UX design and explore its core principles. These principles form the bedrock of your work as a UX designer, guiding your every step, from research to implementation. Ready to discover the cornerstones of UX design? Let's dive in!

UX design, at its essence, is about designing for people. It's about understanding their needs, their behaviors, their emotions, and crafting experiences that resonate with them. Therefore, the core principles of UX design revolve around this central tenet: the user. Here are five key principles to consider:

1. User-centricity: This principle underscores that the user is at the center of every UX design

decision. It means considering the user's needs, wants, and limitations at each stage of the design process. Remember, you're not designing for yourself or your client; you're designing for the user. Empathy, therefore, becomes a crucial tool, enabling you to understand and address the user's perspective.

2. Clarity: A well-designed user experience is one that's clear and intuitive. It means the user should be able to understand how to interact with your product without extensive instructions. The design should guide them through the experience, helping them understand where they are, what they can do, and what's going to happen next. In other words, don't make users think too hard!

3. Consistency: Consistency in UX design means keeping elements uniform throughout the product. It could be related to visual design, like fonts and colors, or interaction design, like how buttons work. Consistency makes the product predictable, making it easier for users to learn and navigate your design.

4. Feedback: In a real-world interaction, actions have immediate reactions. This principle should apply to digital interactions as well. Provide feedback to the user's actions, whether it's a success message after a form submission or a simple color change when a button is clicked. Feedback assures users that the

system is responding to their actions, guiding them through the experience.

5. Simplicity: A good UX design is not one that dazzles users with unnecessary bells and whistles; it's one that makes the user's journey simple and enjoyable. Strive to keep your design as simple as possible, stripping away elements that don't add value. Remember, every additional button, image, or line of text adds cognitive load to the user. Keep it simple, keep it clean.

As we navigate further into the world of UX design, these core principles will serve as your guiding stars. But it's essential to remember that these principles are not isolated pillars; they are interconnected and often influence each other. For instance, achieving clarity might require providing feedback or maintaining consistency. Striving for simplicity might involve a deep understanding of the user's needs.

ux design tools and techniques

We've had quite a journey thus far, exploring the landscape of UX design, its process, and core principles. Now, it's time to equip you with the practical tools and techniques that bring UX design to life. This chapter is your toolshed, brimming with instruments that will help you navigate the intricate maze of UX design. So, let's roll up our sleeves and dig in!

UX design is both an art and a science. As such, it requires a range of tools and techniques for different stages of the design process. While the 'right' tools may vary based on specific project needs, certain staples are broadly used across the industry. Let's explore these tools and understand their role in the UX design process:

1. Research Tools: Research forms the bedrock of the UX design process. Tools like surveys (SurveyMonkey, Google Forms), user interview platforms (Zoom, Microsoft Teams), and analytics tools (Google Analytics, Hotjar) can help you gather valuable user data. Also, qualitative data analysis tools (NVivo, MAXQDA) can assist in interpreting this data and extracting actionable insights.

2. Design and Prototyping Tools: This is where you give form to your research insights. Sketching tools (pen and paper, whiteboards) are great for initial brainstorming and low-fidelity prototyping. For more detailed designs, wireframing and mockup tools like Balsamiq, Sketch, Adobe XD, and Figma are excellent. These tools allow you to create both static designs and interactive prototypes, offering a tangible feel of the final product.

3. User Testing Tools: User testing validates your design with real users. Usability testing platforms like UserTesting, Lookback, and UsabilityHub can help you

conduct remote user tests and gather feedback. These platforms provide video, audio, and sometimes even eye-tracking capabilities to understand how users interact with your design.

4. Collaboration Tools: UX design is a collaborative effort. Tools like Slack or Microsoft Teams for communication, Trello or Asana for project management, and InVision or Figma for design collaboration can streamline the process and foster a cohesive team environment.

In addition to these tools, there are a host of techniques that can help you glean deeper insights, design better solutions, and validate your ideas. Here are a few:

1. Personas: Personas are fictional representations of your target users, based on your research data. They help you empathize with the users and design solutions that cater to their needs.

2. User Journeys and Storyboards: These are visual narratives that depict a user's journey with your product, highlighting their goals, actions, emotions, and touchpoints.

3. Card Sorting: A technique to understand how users categorize information. It can help structure your product's information architecture intuitively.

4. Usability Testing: This involves observing users

interacting with your product and identifying areas of improvement.

Remember, tools and techniques are not an end in themselves; they are a means to an end. The choice of tools and techniques should always be guided by your project's needs and goals. It's about picking the right tool for the right job.

an introduction to project management

defining project management

AFTER EQUIPPING you with a robust UX toolbox, it's time to shift our gaze to another critical aspect of our work—project management. This chapter will serve as your gateway into the captivating world of project management, an invaluable skill for anyone involved in the design process. So, let's set sail!

When we think about project management, we often envision Gantt charts, timelines, and meetings. But, at its heart, project management is fundamentally about navigating complexity. It's about bringing structure to chaos, transforming ideas into reality in the most efficient and effective manner possible.

At its core, project management involves planning, executing, monitoring, controlling, and closing projects. It's about defining clear objectives, managing resources, and ensuring the project's success within the constraints of scope, time, and budget.

Let's break down these elements:

1. Planning: Planning is the compass of project management. It involves defining the project's goals, scope, and deliverables. This step is also where you outline the project timeline, establish the budget, and identify necessary resources. The planning phase is critical—it sets the direction for the entire project.

2. Executing: This phase is where the rubber meets the road. The project team works to deliver the project outputs as per the plan. Executing includes coordinating resources, managing tasks, and maintaining communication among team members.

3. Monitoring: No project runs perfectly according to plan. Monitoring involves tracking the project's progress and performance, comparing them with the plan, and identifying any deviations. This stage is all about maintaining control and ensuring that the project stays on track.

4. Controlling: If monitoring is about identifying deviations, controlling is about taking corrective actions. This phase may involve revising plans, adjusting resources, or even negotiating changes in scope to keep the project on track.

5. Closing: Once the project outputs are delivered,

it's time to formally close the project. This phase involves evaluating the project, documenting lessons learned, and celebrating the team's accomplishments.

It's important to remember that these phases are not strictly sequential—they often overlap and interact in complex ways. And while every project is unique, these phases provide a helpful framework to guide your project management efforts.

As a UX designer, you might wonder, "Why do I need to learn project management? Isn't that the project manager's job?" Here's the thing: while you may not formally carry the title of a 'project manager', as a UX designer, you are invariably managing projects.

Whether you're conducting user research, designing a prototype, or testing a design, you're planning tasks, coordinating resources, and delivering outputs—essentially, you're managing a project.

Mastering project management can help you streamline your design process, coordinate effectively with team members, and deliver better results within time and budget constraints. It enables you to see the big picture, understand how your work fits into the broader project context, and navigate the complexities of real-world projects.

key skills for effective project management

We've been traversing the terrain of project management, getting familiar with its fundamental concepts. Now, it's time to equip ourselves with the essential skills that make for effective project management. This chapter is your training ground to become not just a project participant but a project leader. Let's dive in!

Project management, as we've learned, is a complex endeavor, requiring more than just a keen understanding of the project's goals. It demands a diverse set of skills—skills that allow you to plan, execute, monitor, control, and close projects successfully. Let's explore these skills and understand why they're crucial:

1. Leadership: Project management is, at its heart, a leadership role. It's about guiding your team towards the project's goals, inspiring them, and fostering a positive and collaborative environment. Leadership also entails decision-making—often under uncertainty—and taking responsibility for those decisions.

2. Communication: Effective communication is the lifeblood of project management. It involves clearly articulating project goals, roles, expectations, and feedback. But it's not just about broadcasting information—

it's also about active listening, understanding, and resolving conflicts.

3. Organization: Managing a project requires juggling multiple tasks, deadlines, and resources. Organizational skills—like time management, prioritization, and resource allocation—are crucial to keeping the project on track. It's about bringing order to the chaos.

4. Risk Management: Every project comes with uncertainties and potential risks. Effective project managers can anticipate, identify, and mitigate these risks before they turn into problems. This skill involves analytical thinking, scenario planning, and problem-solving.

5. Adaptability: Projects seldom go exactly as planned. Hence, adaptability—the ability to respond to change, whether it's a change in project scope, resources, or timelines—is a key skill. It's about staying flexible and resilient in the face of the unexpected.

6. Negotiation: Project management often involves balancing conflicting interests—whether it's negotiating scope changes with stakeholders, resource allocation among team members, or deadline extensions. Negotiation skills can help find a middle ground that satisfies all parties involved.

These are not just skills; they're capabilities that you can cultivate and improve over time. They go beyond the realm of project management, enhancing your overall professional persona.

As a UX designer, you might already possess some of these skills. For instance, UX designers are inherently great communicators—communicating design concepts to stakeholders, user needs to the design team, and design feedback to developers. You're also likely to be adept at empathy and active listening, key aspects of communication.

Similarly, UX design demands adaptability—responding to user feedback, changing technology trends, and evolving project needs. The iterative nature of UX design prepares you well for the dynamic world of project management.

As we delve deeper into project management in the coming chapters, we'll see these skills in action. We'll understand how they manifest in the different stages of project management and how you can further hone these skills.

the five stages of project management

In our previous chapters, we've seen the broad landscape of project management and identified the key skills necessary to navigate it effectively. Now, it's time to get up close and personal with the five stages of project management, each a crucial waypoint in our project's journey. Let's take a deeper dive.

Each project, regardless of its nature or complexity, follows a life cycle. It starts as an idea, goes through a series of phases, and ends with the delivery of a product, service, or result. This life cycle is typically divided into five stages: Initiation, Planning, Execution, Monitoring & Control, and Closure. Let's dissect each stage and understand their significance.

1. Initiation: The initiation phase marks the birth of the project. It's where you define the project at a broad level, identifying its purpose, scope, and deliverables. This stage also involves identifying stakeholders, understanding their expectations, and gaining their buy-in. In terms of documentation, the initiation stage usually culminates in a Project Charter, a formal document that defines the project and authorizes its commencement. Remember, a well-defined project is a stepping stone to success.

2. Planning: If initiation gives the project its direction, planning gives it the roadmap. The planning phase involves creating a detailed project plan, including a schedule, budget, and resource allocation. It's about answering the questions of 'what', 'when', 'who', 'how much', and 'how'. Risk assessment, communication plans, and quality assurance procedures are also typically developed at this stage. Armed

with a robust project plan, you and your team can navigate the project terrain with confidence.

3. Execution: Execution is where the plans come to life. In this phase, the project team works on the tasks defined in the project plan, producing the project's deliverables. Regular team meetings, status reports, and communication with stakeholders are key activities during this phase. Remember, execution is not just about doing—it's about doing as per plan.

4. Monitoring & Control: While the execution phase is ongoing, it's essential to have a parallel process that tracks the project's progress and performance. That's where the monitoring and control phase comes in. It involves comparing the project's actual performance with the plan, identifying deviations, and taking corrective actions. It's about ensuring that the project stays on track and delivers as per the expectations.

5. Closure: Once the project's deliverables are complete and accepted by the stakeholders, it's time to formally close the project. The closure phase involves tying up loose ends, conducting a post-project review, documenting lessons learned, and celebrating the team's achievements. While it might seem like a formality, closure is crucial—it's an opportunity to reflect, learn, and improve for future projects.

It's important to remember that these stages are not rigid compartments—they often overlap and interact in complex ways. For instance, you might need to revisit the planning stage during execution, or you might start closure activities for completed parts of the project even while others are still in execution. The key is to understand these stages as a framework, a guide that helps you navigate the project life cycle effectively.

As a UX designer, you'll find that these stages resonate with your design process. Just like a project, a design also goes through similar stages—defining the design problem (Initiation), creating a design plan (Planning), developing the design (Execution), testing and refining the design (Monitoring & Control), and finally, launching the design and reflecting on the process (Closure).

importance of project management in ux design

We've walked a long way together, unraveling the intricacies of project management and its stages. But you might still be wondering, why do UX designers need to concern themselves with project management? Isn't that the project manager's job? Well, the short answer is: project management is everybody's job, especially when you're in a field as dynamic as UX design. This chapter is your key to understanding why project management is essential for you as a UX designer.

UX design and project management, at first glance, may seem like distinct domains. However, upon closer inspection, it becomes clear that they are more intertwined than one might initially presume. In essence, UX design is a project in itself, and applying project management principles can significantly enhance its outcomes.

Let's delve into the reasons why project management is a critical aspect of UX design:

1. Managing Complexity: UX design projects can be complex, involving various stakeholders, tasks, resources, and constraints. Project management provides a framework to manage this complexity, helping you to organize tasks, manage resources, and keep track of deadlines.

2. Delivering Value: UX design is about solving user problems and creating value. Project management ensures that this value is delivered effectively and efficiently. It aligns the project's goals with the stakeholders' expectations and ensures that the project delivers on its promises.

3. Enhancing Collaboration: UX design is a collaborative endeavor, involving designers, developers, business stakeholders, and users. Project management fosters this collaboration, facilitating effective commu-

nication, resolving conflicts, and ensuring everyone is aligned towards the common goal.

4. Navigating Uncertainty: Like any project, UX design involves uncertainty and risks. Project management equips you to manage these uncertainties, anticipate and mitigate risks, and make informed decisions under uncertainty.

5. Learning and Improvement: Project management involves continuous monitoring, feedback, and improvement. It encourages you to reflect on your design process, learn from your successes and failures, and continuously improve your design practice.

But beyond these practical reasons, there's a strategic aspect to why UX designers should embrace project management. Today's professional landscape demands more than just technical or design skills. It requires professionals who can look at the bigger picture, who can lead teams, and who can navigate the complex terrain of modern projects. Project management enables you to fulfill these demands, enhancing your professional persona and career prospects.

As we dive deeper into the intersection of project management and UX design in the subsequent chapters, you'll see these benefits coming to life. You'll see how project management principles can be applied to UX design scenarios, how they can enhance your design process, and how they can help you deliver better design outcomes.

Let's be clear; this journey is not about leaving your design hat and wearing a project management hat. It's about expanding your hat rack, adding more capabilities to your toolkit. It's about evolving from a UX designer to a UX design leader.

3 /
project
management tools
and techniques

traditional project management tools

WE'VE BEEN CHARTING the course of project management, understanding its stages, and appreciating its importance in UX design. Now, it's time to gear up. In this chapter, we'll delve into the toolbox of traditional project management, understanding the tools that have stood the test of time and continue to be relevant in today's digital landscape.

Project management tools are a project manager's best friends. They help in planning, organizing, managing, and controlling projects. They foster collaboration, enhance visibility, and improve productivity. Let's open this toolbox and explore its contents:

1. Gantt Charts: Named after their creator, Henry Gantt, Gantt charts are a staple of project management.

They provide a visual representation of the project schedule, showing tasks, durations, dependencies, and milestones in a timeline view. They are an excellent tool for planning, scheduling, and tracking progress.

2. Critical Path Method (CPM): CPM is a technique for scheduling project activities. It identifies the longest path of tasks in the project, known as the 'critical path'. Any delay in tasks on the critical path directly impacts the project's end date, making this tool critical for managing project timelines.

3. PERT Charts: PERT (Program Evaluation and Review Technique) is another scheduling technique, which focuses on task dependencies and project uncertainties. It represents tasks as nodes and dependencies as arrows, creating a network diagram. It's particularly useful for complex projects with high uncertainty.

4. Work Breakdown Structure (WBS): The WBS is a hierarchical decomposition of the project into manageable chunks, or 'work packages'. It breaks down the project scope into deliverables and sub-deliverables, facilitating scope management, resource allocation, and cost estimation.

5. Risk Matrix: A risk matrix is a tool for risk assessment. It visualizes risks based on their impact and probability, helping you identify high-priority risks and decide on risk responses. It's a crucial tool for proactive risk management.

6. Status Reports: Status reports provide a snapshot of the project's status, covering aspects like progress, issues, risks, and next steps. They are a crucial tool for communication, ensuring that all stakeholders stay informed and aligned.

7. Meetings and Reviews: While not a 'tool' in the traditional sense, meetings and reviews are an essential part of project management. They facilitate communication, collaboration, and decision-making. They include kick-off meetings, team meetings, stakeholder meetings, and review meetings.

These tools, with their roots in traditional project management methodologies, continue to be relevant today. They provide a structured, disciplined approach to managing projects, balancing the creative chaos of UX design with the stability of systematic project management.

agile project management tools

In our last chapter, we explored the realm of traditional project management tools, unearthing invaluable instruments that assist us in structuring and stream-lining our UX projects. But the project management landscape isn't confined to tradition. In the past couple of decades, a new methodology has been making waves, reshaping how we think about and manage projects: Agile.

Agile project management, born in the software industry, is all about flexibility, collaboration, and customer-centricity. It replaces rigid plans with iterative development, bureaucratic hierarchies with self-organizing teams, and hefty documents with working products.

1. Scrum Framework: Scrum is a lightweight Agile framework that advocates iterative development in short cycles called 'Sprints'. Each Sprint starts with a planning meeting, culminates with a review meeting, and is punctuated by daily scrum meetings.

2. Kanban Boards: Kanban is a visual tool for managing workflow. Tasks are represented as cards on a board, which is divided into columns representing workflow stages. As work progresses, cards are moved across the board, providing a visual representation of the workflow.

3. User Stories: In Agile, requirements are captured as user stories, which focus on user needs rather than system features. Each user story encapsulates a small, incremental piece of value and serves as a placeholder for further conversation.

4. Product Backlog: The product backlog is a prioritized list of user stories, representing the evolving understanding of the product. It's continually updated and refined in a process called 'Backlog Grooming'.

5. Burndown Charts: Burndown charts are visual tools for tracking progress. They show the amount of work remaining (usually in terms of story points) against time, providing an at-a-glance view of the project's status.

6. Retrospectives: Retrospectives are a ritual of reflection and learning in Agile. After each iteration, the team gathers to reflect on their experiences, discuss what went well and what didn't, and identify actions for improvement.

7. Velocity: Velocity is a measure of the team's rate of progress. It's calculated as the average amount of work (in story points) completed per iteration. It serves as a guide for future planning and forecasting.

Agile tools are more than just techniques—they are manifestations of Agile values and principles. They foster a collaborative, responsive, and learning-oriented approach, resonating well with the dynamic nature of UX design.

In subsequent chapters, we'll delve deeper into each of these tools, understanding their nuances, their applications in UX design contexts, and digital tools that can aid their implementation.

As we journey through the Agile landscape, keep reflecting on your projects, your challenges, and your successes. Imagine how these Agile tools could revolutionize your design process, how they could make it more responsive, more collaborative, more user-centric.

Remember, Agile is not just about doing things differently—it's about thinking differently. It's about breaking free from rigid plans and embracing change, silencing bureaucratic noise and listening to customers, shifting focus from paperwork to people work.

digital project management tools

Over the past few chapters, we've been touring the project management landscape, exploring traditional and Agile tools. But remember, we are living in a digital age, where cloud-based solutions, mobile applications, and collaborative platforms are the norm. The project management realm is no different. Today, an array of digital project management tools are revolutionizing how we manage projects, offering features that far exceed their analog counterparts.

1. Task Management Tools: Platforms like Trello, Asana, and Jira are revolutionizing how we manage tasks. They offer a digital canvas where you can create, assign, prioritize, and track tasks, making project management a breeze. Their built-in features for labels, attachments, and comments add further value, enhancing collaboration and communication.

2. Collaboration Tools: Collaboration is the bedrock

of modern project management, and tools like Slack and Microsoft Teams are making it seamless. They offer a platform for real-time communication, file sharing, and integration with other tools, fostering collaboration and transparency.

3. Document Management Tools: Managing project documents can be a daunting task. Digital tools like Google Drive, Dropbox, and Confluence offer a solution, providing a cloud-based repository for storing, sharing, and co-editing documents.

4. Time Tracking Tools: Tools like Harvest and Toggl allow for efficient time tracking, enabling you to monitor the time spent on tasks, gain insights into productivity, and make data-driven decisions.

5. Project Portfolio Management Tools: Managing multiple projects? Tools like Monday.com and Project-Manager.com got you covered. They offer dashboards for portfolio management, providing a holistic view of all your projects and facilitating strategic decision-making.

6. Design Collaboration Tools: When it comes to UX design, tools like Figma, Adobe XD, and Sketch are the game-changers. They offer features for design creation, prototyping, collaboration, and user feedback, making the design process more efficient and effective.

These digital tools, with their diverse functionalities, can augment your project management capabilities, making your life as a UX designer easier and your projects more successful.

But remember, each tool has its strengths and weaknesses, and no single tool can be a panacea for all your project management challenges. It's crucial to evaluate your needs, explore your options, and choose the right tools that fit your context. A well-chosen tool can be a force multiplier, but a poorly chosen one can be a bottleneck.

choosing the right tool for your project

As we've journeyed through the landscape of project management tools, from traditional to Agile and then to digital, we've certainly seen an impressive range of options. Each tool offers unique features, benefits, and opportunities. But how do you choose the right tool for your project? That's the conundrum we'll tackle in this chapter.

Choosing the right project management tool isn't just about the tool's features; it's about the alignment between the tool and your project context, team dynamics, and organizational culture. Here are some key factors to consider:

1. Project Complexity: The complexity and scope of your project should be your starting point. Are you managing a small project with a straightforward

process, or is it a complex endeavor with various phases, teams, and dependencies? Different tools are designed to handle different levels of complexity, so choose one that matches your project's scale.

2. Team Size and Distribution: Are you working with a small co-located team, or is your team large and geographically distributed? The latter situation requires tools with robust collaboration features and seamless communication channels.

3. Integration with Existing Systems: Do you already use certain software in your organization, like a CRM system, a file storage platform, or a design tool? If so, choose a project management tool that can integrate with these existing systems to create a unified digital workspace.

4. Usability: Is the tool user-friendly? Can your team quickly learn and adapt to it? The tool's user interface and learning curve are crucial factors. A tool that's hard to use can be a productivity drain rather than a booster.

5. Budget: What's your budget for the project management tool? Remember, costs aren't just about the upfront purchase or subscription fee. Consider the long-term costs of maintenance, upgrades, training, and potential downtime.

6. Support and Community: Does the tool vendor provide reliable customer support? Is there a vibrant

community of users you can turn to for help and advice? These factors can significantly impact your experience with the tool.

These considerations will guide you in making an informed decision. But remember, there's no one-size-fits-all solution. Different projects may require different tools, and that's perfectly fine. What's important is to have a clear understanding of your needs and a willingness to experiment and adapt.

As we navigate this decision-making process, keep reflecting on your projects, your challenges, and your successes. Think about the tools you've used in the past, what worked well and what didn't, and how a new tool can address your current needs and enhance your future projects.

Choosing the right project management tool is a critical step in your UX design journey. It's not just about finding a tool that works; it's about finding a tool that works for you, your team, and your project. It's about finding a tool that empowers you, that enhances your productivity, and that helps you deliver exceptional UX design solutions.

introduction to agile and scrum

agile manifesto: principles and values

WE'VE DELVED into tools and techniques, but let's not forget the importance of mindsets and values. Today, we're going to deep dive into the world of Agile, specifically the Agile Manifesto, which offers principles and values that are crucial for managing projects in a fast-paced, ever-evolving digital environment.

For those uninitiated, Agile emerged as a response to the limitations of traditional project management, particularly in the world of software development. Agile espouses a set of values and principles that prioritize adaptability, collaboration, and customer satisfaction. These are embodied in the Agile Manifesto, a declaration made by a group of software developers in 2001.

The Agile Manifesto comprises four values:

1. Individuals and Interactions Over Processes and Tools: Agile emphasizes the human aspect of software development. It prioritizes team interactions and collaboration over rigid adherence to tools and processes. Remember, tools are facilitators, and processes are guidelines; they should never overshadow the importance of effective human collaboration.

2. Working Software Over Comprehensive Documentation: Agile focuses on delivering a functional product rather than getting tangled in exhaustive documentation. This doesn't imply documentation isn't important; rather, it highlights the emphasis on producing work that adds value and meets user needs.

3. Customer Collaboration Over Contract Negotiation: Agile recognizes the importance of engaging with the customer throughout the project, not just during the initial contract negotiation. Regular feedback loops, openness to change, and shared ownership of the project lead to better outcomes.

4. Responding to Change Over Following a Plan: Agile appreciates the inevitability of change, especially in software development. Rather than strictly

following a set plan, Agile encourages flexibility and adaptation to deliver the best possible product.

These values form the backbone of Agile. But, to translate these values into practice, the Agile Manifesto also outlines 12 principles, some of which include:

- Customer Satisfaction: Deliver valuable software frequently, with a preference for a shorter timescale.

- Welcome Changing Requirements: Agile processes harness change to provide the customer's competitive advantage.

- Deliver Working Software Frequently: Work should be paced to maintain a sustainable speed.

- Business People and Developers Must Work Together Daily: Face-to-face conversation is the most efficient and effective method of conveying information.

- Simplicity: Maximizing the amount of work not done is essential.

- At Regular Intervals, Reflect on How to Become More Effective: Then tune and adjust behavior accordingly.

These principles are not just theoretical concepts. They are practical guidelines that you can implement in your day-to-day project management activities. They help foster a culture of agility, where change is welcomed, collaboration is key, and delivering value to the customer is the primary focus.

As we explore the Agile Manifesto, keep an open mind. Reflect on your own experiences in project management and consider how these Agile values and principles align with them. How can you be more responsive to change? How can you foster more collaboration? How can you deliver more value to your customers?

The Agile Manifesto is more than a statement. It's a philosophy, a mindset, a way of working. It's a beacon guiding us in a complex, uncertain, and volatile world. So, let's embrace Agile. Let's be more adaptive, more collaborative, more customer-centric. Let's continue on our journey, growing, evolving, and mastering the art of project management in the digital age.

agile methodologies: an overview

Now that we've familiarized ourselves with the Agile Manifesto and the underlying principles and values, it's time to understand how these can be practically applied in project management. This leads us to an introduction of various Agile methodologies.

Agile methodologies are approaches that align with the values and principles of the Agile Manifesto. Although they vary in their specifics, all Agile methodologies share the focus on continuous improvement, flexibility, team collaboration, and delivering high-quality results. Now let's take a look at some of the most commonly used Agile methodologies.

First off, we have Scrum. Scrum is arguably the most popular Agile methodology. It divides a project into small work units called 'sprints,' typically lasting 2-4 weeks. At the beginning of each sprint, the team holds a planning meeting to determine what tasks will be completed in that sprint. Each day of the sprint begins with a daily Scrum meeting, or 'stand-up,' to discuss progress and plan for the day. At the end of the sprint, the team reviews the work completed and plans for the next sprint.

Next, we have Kanban. Kanban emphasizes visualizing the work process to limit work-in-progress and maximize efficiency. The team uses a Kanban board, divided into columns representing different stages of the work process. As tasks progress, they move across the board from one column to the next. This visualization helps teams identify bottlenecks and improve their process.

Lean is another Agile methodology that emphasizes efficiency. It focuses on eliminating waste, delivering fast by managing work-in-progress, and deciding as late as possible to provide flexibility. Lean also advocates for empowering the team, building in quality, and optimizing the whole.

Another methodology to discuss is Extreme

Programming (XP). XP places a high emphasis on customer satisfaction and promotes the delivery of high-quality software by introducing practices like pair programming, continuous integration, and test-driven development.

Finally, there's Feature-Driven Development (FDD), which, as the name suggests, organizes software development around making progress on 'features,' or client-valued functions. Unlike other methodologies, FDD requires specific roles and includes five basic activities: develop an overall model, build a features list, plan by feature, design by feature, and build by feature.

By now, you might be wondering, which of these methodologies is the best? The answer, quite honestly, is that it depends. Each methodology has its strengths and is best suited to specific types of projects and teams. The key is to understand the fundamentals of these methodologies and then adapt them as per your team and project needs.

As you explore these methodologies, I encourage you to reflect on your own project management experiences. Which methodologies align with the nature of your projects? Which practices could you incorporate into your work? Remember, Agile is all about learning and adapting, so don't be afraid to experiment and evolve your practices.

understanding scrum: roles, artifacts, and events

You've been introduced to its basic structure in the previous chapter. Now, let's roll up our sleeves and delve deeper into the specific roles, artifacts, and events that make Scrum unique and effective.

First, let's talk about roles. There are three main roles in Scrum: The Product Owner, The Scrum Master, and the Development Team.

The Product Owner is essentially the voice of the customer. This role is responsible for maximizing the value of the product, managing the product backlog, and ensuring that the team is working on the most valuable features. The Product Owner also makes sure that the goals, scope, and product domain are understood by everyone on the Scrum Team.

The Scrum Master, on the other hand, acts as a facilitator and coach for the Scrum Team. They help everyone understand Scrum theory, practices, rules, and values. The Scrum Master is also responsible for removing any obstacles that are hindering the team's progress. They don't manage the team but serve it, creating an environment where the team can be self-organizing and hyper-productive.

The Development Team includes professionals who do the work of delivering a potentially releasable increment of "Done" product at the end of each Sprint. The Development Team in Scrum is self-organizing, cross-functional, and they have collective ownership of the work.

Now, let's move on to Scrum artifacts. These are key pieces of information that the Scrum Team and the stakeholders use to understand the product being developed and its progress.

The Product Backlog is a prioritized list of everything that is known to be needed in the product. It's the single source of requirements for any changes to be made to the product. The Product Owner is responsible for the Product Backlog, including its content, availability, and ordering.

The Sprint Backlog is the set of Product Backlog items selected for the Sprint, plus a plan for delivering the product increment and realizing the Sprint Goal. The Sprint Backlog is a forecast by the Development Team about what functionality will be in the next increment and the work needed to deliver that functionality.

The Increment is the sum of all the Product Backlog items completed during a Sprint and all previous Sprints. At the end of a Sprint, the new increment must be "done," meaning it's in a useable condition and meets the Scrum Team's definition of "done."

Lastly, let's discuss Scrum events. These are specific

activities designed to ensure proper control over the product development. All events are time-boxed, meaning they have a maximum duration.

The Sprint is a time-box of one month or less during which a "done", usable, and potentially releasable product increment is created. It consists of the Sprint Planning, Daily Scrums, the development work, the Sprint Review, and the Sprint Retrospective.

The Sprint Planning is a meeting when the team determines the product backlog items they will work on during that sprint and discusses their initial plan for completing those product backlog items.

Daily Scrum or Stand-Up is a 15-minute event for the Development Team to synchronize activities and create a plan for the next 24 hours.

The Sprint Review happens at the end of the Sprint to inspect the increment and adapt the Product Backlog if needed.

Finally, the Sprint Retrospective occurs after the Sprint Review and before the next Sprint Planning. This is an opportunity for the Scrum Team to inspect itself and create a

plan for improvements to be enacted during the next Sprint.

By now, you can see that Scrum is not merely a methodology but a journey towards improved product development. It promotes a flexible, collaborative working style where a team can focus on delivering value quickly and adjust based on real-time feedback.

scrum in the context of ux design

As we forge ahead in our journey through the terrain of UX Design and Scrum, let's shift our focus onto the intersection of these two domains. Yes, you guessed it right! We will explore how Scrum integrates with UX Design, a marriage of structure and creativity that, when well-executed, can significantly improve the effectiveness of your projects.

Why Scrum and UX?

The agile nature of Scrum and the user-focused approach of UX may seem at odds initially. UX Design often requires substantial up-front user research, whereas Scrum advocates for work being broken down into small, manageable sprints. But, when combined effectively, these two methodologies can complement each other beautifully.

UX practices provide crucial inputs, from user insights to usability evaluations, which can help shape the product backlog and direct the development team's efforts. Meanwhile, Scrum offers a flexible framework that can accommodate the iterative nature of UX Design and provide regular opportunities for user feedback.

UX Roles within Scrum

In the context of Scrum, the UX designer often becomes part of the development team. As a member of this cross-functional team, the designer collaborates closely with developers, testers, and the product owner to ensure that the user perspective is never lost.

UX designers bring their unique skill set to the team, conducting user research, creating personas, designing wireframes and prototypes, conducting usability tests, and continuously iterating based on feedback. Their work informs user stories and acceptance criteria, which then feed into the product backlog.

Incorporating UX Work into Sprints

While some aspects of UX work, like user research and high-level design, might be conducted ahead of the development work, much of the UX design process can fit nicely into Scrum sprints. A sprint could include activities like designing a new feature, conducting a usability test, or iterating on a design based on feedback.

UX tasks can be included in the sprint backlog and managed just like any other tasks. Remember, though, UX work is often iterative and may need to be revisited in future sprints based on user feedback.

Challenges and Solutions

Marrying Scrum and UX design is not without its

challenges. The fast-paced nature of Scrum can sometimes clash with the need for thoughtful, comprehensive design in UX. Balancing speed and quality, managing dependencies between design and development, and accommodating research within the Scrum framework are common challenges.

To tackle these challenges, UX work could start one or two sprints ahead of development, known as 'dual-track Scrum.' This method allows designers to stay ahead, conduct user research, and validate designs while not slowing down the development process.

Another approach is to use design spikes - time-boxed periods dedicated to resolving a design question or problem, which can then inform future work.

To sum it all up, Scrum and UX can indeed work in harmony, with each providing its unique value. It's about ensuring that user needs remain at the heart of development efforts, and that flexibility and responsiveness are built into the design process. It might require some adjustments and a good dose of collaboration, but the results can be well worth it.

implementing scrum in ux design

how scrum can benefit ux projects

YOU'RE TAKING impressive strides in your journey to understand the harmony between Scrum and UX Design. Today, we'll delve into the practical advantages of Scrum and how it can greatly benefit UX projects. By aligning these two concepts, we can create a system that delivers optimal user experiences, meets business goals, and upholds the principles of an agile, responsive methodology.

Scrum's Unique Contribution

The Scrum framework is designed for managing complex, iterative projects. In many ways, it's a perfect fit for UX projects, which are iterative by nature and often involve managing complex interactions and user journeys. Here's how Scrum can contribute to UX projects:

1. Iterative Development: The iterative nature of Scrum is a perfect match for UX design. UX is an iterative process. We design, test, learn, and then iterate. With Scrum, you can fit these cycles into your sprints, allowing for regular user feedback and iterative development. This allows for regular refinement and course correction, leading to a design that's closely aligned with user needs.

2. Transparency and Collaboration: Scrum encourages transparency and collaboration, both of which are critical in UX design. Regular meetings like daily stand-ups and sprint reviews provide a forum for the team to communicate, solve problems, and share progress. This constant communication can lead to a shared understanding of the user and their needs, fostering a user-centered approach across the entire team.

3. Responsiveness to Change: UX Design is a field characterized by change. User preferences change, technology changes, and market trends change. Scrum, with its focus on agility, provides a framework to respond to these changes quickly. Instead of treating changes as setbacks, Scrum allows teams to adapt and incorporate changes into the design process, keeping the product relevant and user-centric.

Enhanced Value Delivery

Scrum enables teams to deliver value early and often through its focus on incremental development. In a UX project, this might mean delivering a functioning prototype early in the project and then continually refining and expanding it based on user feedback. This constant flow of value can lead to higher user satisfaction and better design outcomes.

Moreover, Scrum prioritizes work based on value. The Product Owner, in collaboration with the team and stakeholders, prioritizes the product backlog based on the value that each item brings. This value-driven approach ensures that the team is always working on the most impactful tasks, leading to efficient use of resources and a design that delivers maximum value to the user.

Risk Reduction

Risk is inherent in any project, and UX projects are no exception. Whether it's the risk of designing a product that doesn't meet user needs, or the risk of scope creep, project risks can be damaging if not managed well. Scrum can help reduce these risks.

By breaking down the work into sprints, Scrum allows for risks to be identified and addressed early. Regular retrospectives provide an opportunity for the team to reflect on what's working and what's not and to take corrective action.

Moreover, by delivering increments of the product regularly, Scrum reduces the risk of ending up with a product that doesn't meet user needs. Each increment can be tested and feedback can be used to improve subsequent iterations.

In the Bigger Picture

Bringing Scrum and UX Design together is an exercise in balancing structure and flexibility, rigour and creativity. When done well, it can lead to designs that not only meet user needs but also adapt to changes and deliver continual value.

While it's not without its challenges, the benefits of using Scrum for UX projects are substantial. The key is to keep the lines of communication open, embrace change, and always, always keep the user at the center of everything you do.

case study: successful scrum implementation in ux design

Right, let's break down a real-world application of Scrum in UX design. We're going to walk you through a case study that highlights a successful Scrum implementation, showcasing the transformative power of Agile project management.

We'll call our company "InspireTech." InspireTech is a leading software development company that designs and builds mobile apps for various clients. While InspireTech had always been renowned for its creativity and technical prowess, it had been encountering issues with its old waterfall approach to project management.

InspireTech was struggling with long development cycles, frequent scope creep, and a lack of customer satisfaction due to insufficient involvement and feedback during the development process. They knew a change was necessary. That change took the form of the Scrum methodology.

Step 1: Establishing the Scrum Team

The first thing InspireTech did was to form a Scrum team for a new project. The project's goal was to develop a mobile app for a client in the hospitality industry. The Scrum Team consisted of a Scrum Master, a Product Owner, and a cross-functional Development Team of UX designers, developers, and testers.

Step 2: Creating the Product Backlog

The Product Owner, in collaboration with stakeholders, developed a product backlog. This backlog was a comprehensive list of features and functions needed for the app, ranked by their value to the end-user and business. User stories were written for each feature, describing the functionality from an end-user perspective.

Step 3: Sprint Planning

In the sprint planning meeting, the Scrum team selected user stories from the product backlog to be completed during the first sprint. They agreed on a sprint goal - to create a functional prototype of the main user interface.

Step 4: The Sprint

Over the next two weeks, the Development Team held daily Scrum meetings to discuss progress, clarify requirements, and address any issues or roadblocks. The Scrum Master facilitated these meetings and worked tirelessly to remove any impediments. The Product Owner was readily available to answer questions and make quick decisions.

The UX designers focused on creating user-centered designs, iterating on feedback from the Product Owner and the rest of the team. They developed wireframes and interactive prototypes, which they tested and improved continuously.

Step 5: Sprint Review and Retrospective

At the end of the Sprint, the team presented the functional prototype during the Sprint Review. The stakeholders, including the client, were able to provide feedback directly, which was incorporated into the product backlog.

Following the Sprint Review, the team held a Sprint Retrospective. They reflected on what went well, what could be improved, and agreed on changes to implement in the next Sprint.

The Outcome

By adopting Scrum, InspireTech transformed their development process. The team was able to deliver value continuously, with the client engaged and providing feedback every step of the way. This ensured that the end product was exactly what the client wanted, resulting in high customer satisfaction.

Moreover, the UX designers found that Scrum enabled them to validate their designs faster, with real-time feedback allowing for rapid iterations. They were able to work more efficiently and effectively, producing work that truly met the users' needs.

In summary, Scrum brought a significant improvement in collaboration, efficiency, and satisfaction for all parties involved. It fostered a flexible, adaptive approach, allowing the InspireTech team to deliver a superior product aligned with their client's vision.

This case study showcases how the principles and processes of Scrum can be applied successfully in the context of UX design. It provides a practical example of how Scrum facilitates collaboration, improves productivity, and ultimately leads to a better product.

challenges of implementing scrum in ux and how to overcome them

Shifting gears from our recent case study, let's discuss the potential challenges when implementing Scrum in UX and, of course, the strategies to navigate these hurdles. It's important to understand that while Scrum can yield tremendous benefits, like all good things, it's not without its difficulties. But don't worry, we'll also delve into how these can be addressed effectively.

Challenge 1: Aligning UX Design with Sprints

One of the key challenges is the difficulty of aligning UX design work with the strict timelines of a Scrum Sprint. Design is a creative and often unpredictable process that can't always be neatly packaged into two-week increments.

Overcoming Challenge 1

One effective way to address this is by adopting a dual-track Scrum approach, where discovery (user research and design) and delivery (development and testing) happen concurrently but as separate tracks. The UX designers can stay one or two sprints ahead of the developers, allowing for the unpredictability of the design process while still aligning with the overall project timeline.

Challenge 2: Collaborative Decision Making

Another challenge is the need for collaborative decision-making in Scrum, which can be a departure from traditional design processes. UX designers may be used to having the final say on design decisions, but in Scrum, these decisions need to be made collaboratively with the entire team.

Overcoming Challenge 2

Open communication and trust-building exercises can go a long way in promoting effective collaboration. Regularly involving the whole team in design discussions and reviews can foster a shared understanding and create a sense of joint ownership over the product.

Challenge 3: User Feedback and Iterations

Scrum's fast-paced nature can make it difficult to gather comprehensive user feedback and implement design changes within a sprint.

Overcoming Challenge 3

UX designers can employ lean UX principles to make quick, iterative changes based on minimum viable tests. Also, consider introducing staggered user testing and feedback sessions throughout the project, not just at the end of each sprint, to ensure user insights are continuously informing the design.

Challenge 4: Handling Scope Creep

Changes and additions to the project scope can be a significant challenge in Scrum, especially when they come in the middle of a sprint. This can disrupt the workflow and make it hard to complete committed user stories on time.

Overcoming Challenge 4

Having a well-defined and prioritized product backlog can significantly reduce scope creep. Regular backlog grooming sessions with the Product Owner and the entire Scrum team can ensure that everyone is on the same page and the most valuable user stories are always being worked on.

Challenge 5: Sufficient Design Documentation

In Scrum, the focus is on delivering working software rather than extensive documentation. This might make some designers uncomfortable as they may be accustomed to creating detailed design specifications.

Overcoming Challenge 5

Instead of extensive design documentation, lean on interactive prototypes, wireframes, and other visual tools. They can effectively communicate design intent and reduce the need for comprehensive design specifications.

And that wraps up our discussion on the challenges of implementing Scrum in UX. Remember, Scrum isn't a magic wand that instantly eliminates all project-related challenges. It is, however, a robust framework that, when correctly adapted to your UX design process, can lead to more efficient workflows, better team collaboration, and ultimately, a product that meets user needs.

advanced scrum practices for ux design

scrum ceremonies and ux: fitting the pieces together

THE JOURNEY into the fusion of Scrum and UX design continues, and today's focus is on the integration of UX design activities into Scrum ceremonies. If you're wondering how the rituals of Scrum can accommodate the fluidity of UX design, you're in the right place. Let's delve into this exciting topic!

Sprint Planning and UX

Sprint planning is the initial ceremony in Scrum, where the team determines the scope of work to be tackled during the upcoming sprint. Herein, the product owner, Scrum master, and development team discuss and agree on the goals, backlog items, and the plan of attack.

From a UX perspective, sprint planning is a crucial opportunity to ensure that user needs and experiences drive the decisions made. UX designers can participate by sharing research insights about user needs and expectations. They can also provide design guidelines, wireframes, or prototypes that have been developed to address these needs. This involvement helps ensure the work prioritized aligns with the user's perspective, thus helping to steer the sprint towards a user-centric direction.

Daily Scrum and UX

The daily scrum, also known as the daily stand-up, is a brief meeting for the Scrum team to synchronize their work and plan for the next 24 hours. For UX designers, this is an excellent time to share updates about ongoing design work, such as results from usability testing or modifications made to designs based on feedback. The daily scrum encourages transparency and ongoing communication, helping to keep the entire team informed about design decisions and progress.

Sprint Review and UX

The sprint review happens at the end of each sprint, where the Scrum team and stakeholders inspect the increment of work done. The team presents the finished backlog items and demonstrates the functionality. In terms of UX, this is a crucial moment for designers to showcase their work, gather feedback, and align with stakeholders. Feedback from these meetings can directly feed into future iterations, keeping the design relevant and user-centric.

Sprint Retrospective and UX

The sprint retrospective is the final Scrum ceremony in each sprint, providing an opportunity for the team to reflect and learn. UX designers can contribute by sharing what worked and what didn't in the design process, just as other team members will do the same from their perspectives. This feedback can lead to process adjustments that can make the next sprint more efficient and effective.

The Intersection of Scrum and UX Design

As you can see, each Scrum ceremony offers unique opportunities for integrating UX activities and perspectives. In sprint planning, UX insights help to prioritize user-driven goals; in daily scrums, UX updates facilitate team-wide understanding; in sprint reviews, UX deliverables are inspected and validated; and in sprint retrospectives, UX experiences contribute to team learning and continuous improvement.

Fitting UX into Scrum ceremonies isn't about shoe-horning one process into another. Instead, it's about aligning two complementary perspectives—user-centric design and agile development—around a shared goal: delivering valuable, usable, and delightful experiences to the user.

The beauty of Scrum lies in its flexibility. It's a framework that encourages teams to adapt it to their specific context. So, if you're a UX designer in a Scrum team, don't feel pressured to stick to traditional interpretations of these ceremonies. Instead, leverage these events to foster collaboration, promote understanding of user needs, and drive the creation of a product that will truly resonate with its users.

incorporating user testing in scrum sprints

In our journey to integrate User Experience (UX) into the Scrum framework, we've tackled a lot of ground. Today, we are focusing on a crucial topic, one that helps us validate our designs and ensure we're building the right product - user testing in Scrum sprints.

Why User Testing Matters

Let's start by reiterating why user testing is vital. User testing allows us to evaluate our product by observing real users interacting with it. This step is crucial because it uncovers issues that were not visible to us, allowing us to iterate and improve the product before launch. Skipping user testing may lead to a product that does not meet the needs of users, even if it meets the initial requirements.

The Challenge with User Testing in Scrum

Scrum sprints usually last between one to four weeks, during which the team plans, designs, builds, tests, and reviews a product increment. Due to this short timeline, it might seem challenging to incorporate user testing in the mix. Yet, integrating user testing into Scrum sprints is not only possible but also beneficial. The trick lies in efficient planning and execution.

Plan User Testing Beforehand

The first step to integrate user testing into a Scrum sprint is planning ahead. At the end of a sprint, once we know what will be developed in the next sprint, we can plan the user testing activities. This could include deciding on the testing method, the user tasks, and the user profiles for recruitment. The earlier these activities are planned, the smoother the process will be.

Conduct User Testing Early and Often

The ideal time to conduct user testing is as soon as there is a testable product. In a Scrum context, this could mean testing early versions of the product or prototype within the sprint. The earlier we test, the quicker we can get feedback, allowing the team to make necessary adjustments within the sprint.

Also, instead of conducting one large testing session, consider several smaller ones. This approach allows for quick feedback loops and more manageable changes.

Analyze and Incorporate the Feedback

After conducting the tests, the next step is to analyze the results and share them with the team. In a Scrum environment, this could take place during the daily Scrum or a specially scheduled meeting. The key here is to turn the feedback into actionable backlog items. These could be new features, adjustments to existing features, or bug fixes.

A Final Note

Including user testing in your Scrum sprints may feel like an additional layer of complexity at first. However, when implemented effectively, it can be a valuable tool to ensure that the product you're developing truly meets the needs of your users. Plus, it can save your team from potential pitfalls and costly mistakes down the line.

Remember, the ultimate goal of both Scrum and UX design is to create a product that provides value to the users. Therefore, integrating user testing into Scrum sprints is a strategic move that aligns with this shared goal.

maintaining user focus in scrum environments

We've been traversing a captivating journey, diving into the exciting world of Scrum and User Experience (UX) design. We've learned about Scrum, its core elements, and how user testing can be incorporated into your sprints. Now, it's time to understand how to maintain a user focus throughout the Scrum process.

Understanding the Importance of User Focus

Before we begin, let's underline why it's crucial to maintain a user focus in a Scrum environment. Remember, the ultimate goal of Scrum and UX design is to create a product that delivers value to the end-user. This is best achieved when the entire team understands the users, their needs, their behaviors, and their expectations. Maintaining a user focus ensures that we don't just build things right, but we build the right things.

Embedding User Focus in User Stories

One of the best ways to ensure user focus in a Scrum environment is through the creation of user stories. User stories are a fundamental aspect of Scrum. They define what a user needs to achieve and why, acting as a placeholder for conversation about these needs. When well written, user stories keep the user at the heart of the conversation, helping to define the product backlog and, subsequently, the sprint backlog.

Each user story is generally written from the perspective of a user and follows a simple structure: "As a (type of user), I want (some goal) so that (some reason)." This format helps to anchor each feature or requirement in the needs and wants of the user, promoting user-focused discussions within the Scrum team.

Maintaining User Focus in the Backlog Grooming and Sprint Planning

Maintaining a user focus shouldn't stop at the creation of user stories. It should extend to all Scrum activities, including backlog grooming and sprint planning. During these sessions, it's vital to continually ask questions such as "How does this benefit the user?" or "What user problem does this solve?" By keeping these questions in mind, we ensure that user needs are always at the forefront of our decision-making process.

Consider User Feedback in Retrospective Meetings

Scrum encourages iterative development and continual learning. This philosophy extends to learning about our users. During the sprint retrospective, take the time to discuss what you've learned about the user during the sprint. What worked? What didn't? What surprises came up during user testing? This will help your team adapt and improve your understanding of the user with each sprint.

Fostering a User-focused Culture

Ultimately, maintaining user focus in a Scrum environment goes beyond specific practices or techniques. It's about fostering a user-focused culture within your team and organization. This means continually reminding everyone that whatever they're working on, be it a new feature or a bug fix, it's all in the service of creating a better product for the user.

7 /

the role of a ux designer in project management

ux designer as a project manager: key responsibilities

AS WE CONTINUE to weave the intricate web of UX design and project management, let's now turn our gaze toward a compelling scenario - what happens when a UX designer dons the mantle of a project manager? How does this dual role affect the project and its outcomes? And importantly, what are the key responsibilities when managing this dual role? Let's find out!

Wearing Two Hats

One might ask, is it possible or even desirable for a UX designer to take on project management duties? The answer is: absolutely! Small teams or startup environments often require team members to wear multiple hats. As UX designers, we possess an inherent understanding of the user, which when coupled with project management skills, can lead to outcomes that are tightly aligned with user needs.

Understanding the User and the Project

As a UX designer turned project manager, your primary responsibility is maintaining a dual focus. You're not just considering the project from the user's perspective, but also from a broad project perspective. It's a dance between understanding the minutiae of user needs and the larger project goals. Your role is to ensure that each step of the project aligns with user expectations without losing sight of the project's scope, budget, and timeline.

Clear Communication

Communication is the lifeblood of any project, and even more so when you're managing the dual roles of UX designer and project manager. You need to ensure that every team member understands the user's needs, how these inform the design decisions, and how they fit into the larger project goals.

You're also the link between stakeholders and the team. Translating user needs and design concepts into language that stakeholders can understand and align with is essential. It's about bridging the gap between user empathy and business objectives.

Balancing User Advocacy and Project Needs

It's easy for a UX designer to become engrossed in advocating for the user. But as a project manager, it's equally crucial to remember the project's constraints and business objectives. Balancing user advocacy and project needs is a crucial aspect of this dual role.

For instance, you might champion a feature that users will love, but it might be too expensive or time-consuming to implement. In this case, it's your responsibility to find a compromise that satisfies both user needs and project constraints.

Leading the Team

One of the key responsibilities as a project manager is leading the team. Here, your deep understanding of the user and the project comes in handy. Leading the team involves aligning everyone's work with the user's needs, project goals, and timelines.

Your leadership will also entail creating an environment where everyone feels their work contributes to the project's success and ultimately enhances the user experience.

Managing Resources

Another key responsibility in this dual role is resource management. This not only means managing the team's time but also the project's budget and any other resources at your disposal. You need to ensure resources are allocated in a way that maximizes value for the user while staying within the project's limits.

Keeping an Eye on the Big Picture

As a UX designer, it's easy to get lost in the details of design. However, as a project manager, you must also keep an eye on the big picture. This includes the project's overall timeline, the business goals, market trends, and the competitive landscape.

navigating team dynamics

In our previous chapters, we've explored the intriguing symbiosis of UX design and project management. Today, we delve into another crucial aspect of this relationship – navigating team dynamics. As the person straddling the roles of a UX designer and a project manager, understanding and guiding team dynamics becomes one of your key responsibilities. Let's take a closer look at how you can effectively navigate this delicate yet essential aspect.

The Significance of Team Dynamics

Before diving in, it's important to understand why team dynamics matter so much. A harmonious and productive team is akin to a well-oiled machine. When everyone is in sync and focused on common goals, the output is naturally high-quality, and the project progresses smoothly. Conversely, poor team dynamics can lead to conflicts, inefficiencies, and a decline in the quality of work, often leading to project delays or failures. Thus, steering team dynamics is a crucial aspect of your role.

Knowing Your Team

As with UX design, the first step in navigating team dynamics is understanding your users, which in this case, are your team members. Everyone has unique working styles, strengths, weaknesses, communication preferences, and motivational triggers. Understanding these aspects allows you to assign roles efficiently, resolve conflicts proactively, and keep everyone motivated.

Creating a Collaborative Environment

A key aspect of positive team dynamics is collaboration. As the team's leader, you need to create an environment where everyone feels comfortable sharing ideas, asking questions, and providing constructive feedback. Regular team meetings, brainstorming sessions, and open lines of communication can help foster this collaborative spirit. This not only encourages creative problem-solving but also helps build a stronger, more cohesive team.

Promoting Clear Communication

Clear communication is the cornerstone of successful team dynamics. It's your responsibility to ensure that every team member understands their roles, the project objectives, and how their work contributes to the overall user experience. Equally, it's crucial to keep the team updated on project progress, any changes in plans, and feedback from stakeholders. This level of transparency reduces confusion, builds trust, and ensures everyone is aligned towards the same goals.

Managing Conflict

Conflict is inevitable in any team, but it needn't be detrimental. Healthy conflict can lead to better ideas, solutions, and team cohesion, provided it's managed effectively. As a project manager, it's your role to mediate conflicts, ensuring they are resolved in a respectful and constructive manner. Remember, the goal is not to avoid conflict, but to navigate it in a way that benefits the team and the project.

Motivating the Team

Motivation is a key driver of productivity and quality. As a team leader, you need to understand what motivates each team member and leverage this to keep them engaged and driven. This could be recognition, opportunities for growth, creative freedom, or a combination of these. Regular check-ins, positive feedback, and recognition of good work go a long way in keeping the team motivated.

Adapting to Change

Projects are dynamic, with changes in requirements, timelines, and resources being the norm rather than the exception. Adaptability, therefore, is a crucial part of team dynamics. As a team leader, it's your role to help the team navigate these changes without impacting productivity or the team's morale. This involves clear communication, adequate training, and sometimes, redefining roles and responsibilities.

Navigating team dynamics may seem daunting, but with understanding, empathy, and effective communication, it can become one of the most rewarding aspects of your dual role as a UX designer and a project manager. It not only leads to successful projects but also to personal growth and strong, productive relationships with your team members.

communicating with stakeholders: tips and techniques

After exploring the nuances of team dynamics in our previous chapter, we're now going to focus on another crucial aspect of your role as a UX designer-turned-project manager – communicating effectively with stakeholders. Stakeholder communication, while challenging, is essential for any project's success. Let's delve into how to do it right.

Who are the Stakeholders?

Stakeholders include anyone who has an interest in the project or who is affected by its outcome. This can range from clients, senior management, and project sponsors, to end-users and even your own team members. Each group has its own set of expectations, priorities, and communication preferences, making it crucial for you to tailor your communication strategy accordingly.

Understanding Stakeholder Expectations

Understanding stakeholder expectations is the first step towards effective communication. Each stakeholder will have a different set of expectations based on their role and involvement in the project. It's crucial to identify these early on, as they can significantly impact the direction and priorities of the project. Regular check-ins, feedback sessions, and open discussions can help you gauge and manage these expectations effectively.

Setting Clear Objectives

Once you understand stakeholder expectations, the next step is to set clear project objectives. This involves communicating the project's purpose, scope, timelines, and deliverables in a way that is easily understandable to all stakeholders. Setting clear objectives not only ensures everyone is on the same page, but also provides a solid framework for all project-related decisions and discussions.

Choosing the Right Communication Channels

Choosing the right communication channels for each stakeholder group is key. While some stakeholders may prefer regular email updates, others might want to be involved in project meetings or prefer a quick phone call. Understanding their preferences and availability can make the communication process smoother and more efficient.

Regular Updates and Progress Reports

Providing regular updates and progress reports is an essential part of stakeholder communication. This keeps stakeholders informed about the project's status, any changes in plans, and potential issues that might impact the project. Additionally, regular updates show stakeholders that their input and involvement are valued, building trust and fostering better relationships.

Managing Feedback and Criticism

Feedback and criticism, both positive and negative, are part and parcel of any project. As a project manager, you'll need to be adept at managing this. Always be open to feedback, and consider it as an opportunity for improvement. Also, remember to communicate any changes or adaptations made based on this feedback to the stakeholders, showing them that their input is valuable and actioned upon.

Empathy in Communication

At the end of the day, effective communication boils down to empathy. Understanding the concerns, priorities, and perspectives of your stakeholders can greatly enhance the quality and effectiveness of your communication. Whether it's managing expectations, responding to feedback, or discussing changes in plans, empathy can help you navigate these conversations in a respectful and constructive manner.

Communicating effectively with stakeholders is a delicate balance of information, empathy, and adaptability. It's an art that you'll continually refine as you progress in your role. But remember, the effort you put into it pays off manifold, not just in terms of project success, but also in building strong, positive relationships with your stakeholders.

balancing ux design and project management

managing time and resources effectively

WE'VE JUST FINISHED an enriching discussion on effective communication with stakeholders. Now, let's shift our focus to an equally pivotal aspect of project management - managing time and resources effectively. As UX designers stepping into the shoes of project managers, you'll soon discover that time and resources are two of your most valuable assets. Utilizing them efficiently can mean the difference between a project's success or failure. Let's delve deeper into this intriguing topic.

Understanding the Time-Resource Dynamic

At the outset, it's essential to understand the dynamic between time and resources. Simply put, time is the duration needed to complete the project, and resources refer to everything you'll need during that time, such as personnel, equipment, and budget. The two are intricately linked - a change in one often impacts the other. Hence, effectively managing both is crucial.

Creating a Project Schedule

The first step towards managing time effectively is creating a detailed project schedule. This schedule should include key milestones, tasks, their dependencies, and estimated completion times. Remember to factor in buffers for unexpected delays. A well-planned schedule provides a roadmap for the project and keeps the team aligned.

Resource Planning

After defining the schedule, resource planning comes into play. This involves identifying what resources you need, when you need them, and how you'll use them. Resource planning also includes contingency planning for unexpected situations, like a team member falling sick or a sudden budget cut. Adequate planning ensures resources are available when required, preventing bottlenecks that could derail the project.

Prioritization

With numerous tasks and limited resources, prioritization becomes essential. Not all tasks are created equal; some are more critical to project progress than others. By prioritizing tasks based on their impact and urgency, you can ensure that important tasks are completed first, even if unexpected issues arise.

Delegation

As a project manager, you can't do everything yourself – and that's where delegation comes in. Delegating tasks not only saves you time but also empowers your team members and makes the best use of their skills. Remember, effective delegation involves trust, clear communication of expectations, and provision for necessary support.

Monitoring and Adjusting

Creating a schedule and resource plan is just the beginning. Regular monitoring and adjustment are crucial for effective management. Track the project's progress against the schedule, evaluate resource usage, and make adjustments as needed. Regular monitoring allows you to spot issues early and adjust plans before they become major problems.

Using Time and Resource Management Tools

Several digital tools can aid in managing time and resources. From project management software like Jira or Trello to time tracking tools like TimeDoctor, these can automate tasks, provide visualizations of progress, and ensure more accurate tracking.

Developing a Resourceful Mindset

Lastly, it's essential to develop a resourceful mindset. This means thinking creatively, problem-solving, and making the most of what you have. Sometimes, effective resource management isn't just about using resources efficiently, but also about maximizing their potential.

Successfully managing time and resources is no small feat. It requires planning, monitoring, adjusting, and a dash of creativity. But with practice and experience, you'll find your stride. And remember, every challenge you overcome is another step forward in your journey as a successful UX designer-turned-project manager.

prioritizing tasks and user needs

We've recently delved into the vital aspects of time and resource management. As we continue our journey through project management in UX design, let's now address another fundamental topic - prioritizing tasks and user needs. Prioritization is the magic ingredient that can streamline your project roadmap, keep your team focused, and ensure that you're delivering the greatest value to your users. Let's unpack how this process works.

The Importance of Prioritization

In an ideal world, we'd have infinite resources to

complete every task and meet every user need immediately. In reality, our time, manpower, and budgets are finite. This scarcity necessitates prioritization - determining the order of tasks based on their importance and urgency. Good prioritization balances immediate project needs, long-term goals, and user expectations. It ensures that we focus our energy and resources where they can make the most significant impact.

Task Prioritization in Practice

Let's start with task prioritization. Every project is composed of myriad tasks. Some are critical path tasks, essential to move the project forward. Others, while useful, don't carry the same weight.

One useful tool for prioritizing tasks is the Eisenhower Matrix, named after President Dwight D. Eisenhower. This matrix divides tasks into four categories: Urgent and Important, Not Urgent but Important, Urgent but Not Important, and Not Urgent or Important.

Tasks in the Urgent and Important quadrant are your top priority, while those in the Not Urgent or Important category can usually be deferred or even eliminated. This method forces a conscious evaluation of each task, leading to more effective prioritization.

Prioritizing User Needs

Alongside tasks, we must also prioritize user needs.

After all, the goal of UX design is to deliver a product that meets those needs effectively.

User needs can be gathered through various channels, including user research, feedback, and usability testing. Once collected, you'll likely find that not all user needs are equal. Some are fundamental, tied to the core utility of your product. Others may be peripheral, enhancing the user experience but not integral to it.

To prioritize user needs, consider factors like the need's prevalence among your user base, its impact on user satisfaction, and its alignment with your business goals. This evaluation can help you determine which needs should be addressed first.

Balancing Task Priorities and User Needs

Now, here's the real challenge – balancing task priorities with user needs. Sometimes, these will align neatly. A high-priority task may directly address a top user need. In other cases, you may need to juggle task deadlines with evolving user expectations.

Remember, good project management isn't about rigidly sticking to a plan; it's about adapting to changes without losing sight of your end goals. Maintaining a dialogue with your team, staying attuned to user feedback, and being willing to reassess your priorities can help you strike this balance.

The Power of Prioritization

Effective prioritization can empower your project

and your team. It provides clarity, reduces overwhelm by highlighting where focus should be directed, and ensures alignment with your users' needs. In short, it's a driver of efficiency, satisfaction, and ultimately, project success.

To summarize, mastering prioritization in both tasks and user needs is an art that UX designers transitioning to project managers should strive to acquire. It's an ongoing process of learning and fine-tuning, but with persistence, you can turn it into a powerful tool in your project management toolkit.

case study: effective balance of ux design and project management

Let's continue our adventure by taking a step back from theory and stepping into the real world. As we've spent quite some time discussing the principles of project management in UX design, now it's time to look at a case where these principles were applied effectively. We'll be examining how an e-commerce platform managed to strike the right balance between UX design and project management.

Background

Our case study centers around an established e-commerce platform, we'll call it ShopOnline. With growing customer expectations and competition, Shop-

Online's management decided to revamp their website to enhance their customer experience. The project's goal was to design a more intuitive, easy-to-navigate website that would reduce cart abandonment rates and increase sales.

Setting the Stage

When ShopOnline started this project, they realized the need to maintain a fine balance between UX design and project management. The UX designers were tasked with understanding user needs and designing the platform accordingly, while project managers were responsible for coordinating between teams, managing resources, and ensuring timely project delivery. The challenge was to ensure these roles worked together harmoniously to deliver the project's desired outcomes.

The Process

The project kicked off with user research, as it was crucial to understand what customers wanted from the platform. The UX team conducted interviews, surveys, and usability testing with current and potential users. At the same time, project managers collaborated with the UX team to define the project scope, set timelines, and allocate resources effectively.

The results of the user research led to the identification of key areas for improvement - product search functionality, navigation, and the checkout process. The UX team started working on the design changes, keeping these user needs in focus. They also ensured frequent user testing to validate their design choices.

Meanwhile, project managers used their task prioritization skills to identify which improvements were most critical. For example, as the checkout process was identified as the main reason for cart abandonment, the tasks associated with revamping it were marked as high-priority.

Challenges and Solutions

As is typical in any project, ShopOnline faced several challenges. One significant issue was incorporating user feedback into the design without causing project delays. For instance, during user testing, some users suggested adding a product comparison feature. This feature wasn't in the original project scope, and incorporating it would require extra time and resources.

Here, the skills we discussed in prioritizing tasks and user needs came into play. The project management and UX design team held a meeting to discuss this feedback. They considered the potential value this feature would add for the users and weighed it against the additional resources and time required. They decided to include this feature, acknowledging its importance for user satisfaction, and adjusted the project timeline and tasks accordingly.

Outcomes

Thanks to effective collaboration between the project management and UX design teams, ShopOnline successfully launched its revamped website. The new site was well-received by users, and within six months, they saw a significant decrease in cart abandonment rates and a corresponding increase in sales.

This case study highlights the effective balance of UX design and project management. ShopOnline managed to deliver a project that not only met its business objectives but also significantly improved the user experience. The key was constant collaboration and communication between the UX and project management teams, coupled with a shared commitment to user needs and project goals.

As we conclude this chapter, remember that the marriage of UX design and project management is a dynamic one. It's about keeping an open mind, communicating, and being ready to make decisions that best serve both the users and the project. As we continue on our journey, we'll explore more tools and techniques that can help you manage UX projects more effectively. Stay tuned as we move towards our next stop – managing project risks in UX design.

This will give you even more insight and tools to take your UX project management skills to the next level!

9 /
future of ux design and project management

emerging trends in ux design and project management

AS WE'VE JOURNEYED through UX design and project management's intertwining landscapes, we've established some important concepts, principles, and techniques that are integral to this field. However, much like the digital world, UX design and project management are dynamic, evolving disciplines that continue to adapt and transform. In this chapter, let's explore some of the emerging trends that are currently shaping the field and how they're adding new layers to our ongoing conversation on managing UX projects.

Designing for Voice User Interface (VUI)

The rise of smart speakers and virtual assistants like Amazon's Alexa and Google Assistant has made voice user interfaces (VUIs) a significant area of focus in UX design. VUIs present a unique challenge - how to create an intuitive, engaging user experience without a visual component. As such, UX designers are increasingly required to consider voice interactions in their designs.

From a project management perspective, incorporating VUIs adds a new dimension to the planning and execution of UX projects. It calls for a deeper understanding of natural language processing, speech recognition technology, and audio design, which may require collaboration with new team members and stakeholders. Furthermore, user testing for VUIs demands unique approaches, such as testing for different accents, languages, and voice tones.

Artificial Intelligence in UX Design

AI is making its mark on every field, and UX design is no exception. AI-driven design tools are enhancing the efficiency of the design process, offering capabilities like automated design generation based on user data. Moreover, AI-powered chatbots and recommendation engines are becoming a staple in user interfaces, contributing to more personalized user experiences.

Project managers need to consider the implications of AI on resource allocation, team collaboration, and project timelines. The incorporation of AI in a project may necessitate working with data scientists, machine learning engineers, and AI specialists, making interdisciplinary collaboration more crucial than ever.

Augmented Reality (AR) and Virtual Reality (VR)

AR and VR are pushing the boundaries of immersive user experiences. They present unique opportunities for UX designers to craft interfaces that blend digital and physical worlds. For instance, in an e-commerce app, AR could allow users to virtually 'try on' clothes or place furniture in their room.

However, designing for AR and VR requires specialized skills and technologies. Project managers must account for this in their planning, potentially bringing in experts in 3D modeling, AR/VR development, and spatial design. The testing phase may also require specialized equipment and methodologies.

Remote Collaboration

The global shift towards remote work has had a profound impact on how teams collaborate on UX projects. Remote collaboration tools are rapidly evolving to meet these new demands, offering features like real-time design collaboration, virtual whiteboards, and remote usability testing.

Project managers need to adapt to this remote work environment, ensuring clear communication and effective collaboration among distributed team members. They need to establish remote working protocols, manage different time zones, and leverage digital tools to keep the project on track.

As these trends continue to shape the landscape of UX design and project management, they inevitably add complexity to our conversation. But, they also present exciting opportunities to create more innovative, engaging, and impactful user experiences.

the impact of technology on ux design and project management

We're going to take a step back and consider the broader impact of technology on both UX design and project management as a whole.

Technological Influence on UX Design

To understand the impact of technology on UX design, we need to recall why UX design exists in the first place: to create meaningful, enjoyable experiences for users interacting with a product or service. Technology influences UX design by continually expanding the boundaries of these interactions and the mediums through which they occur.

Consider, for example, the transition from web to mobile. As technology evolved and smartphones became ubiquitous, UX designers had to adapt their strategies to consider smaller screen sizes, touch controls, and mobile-specific use cases. Fast forward to the present day, and UX designers are faced with designing for smart watches, voice interfaces, and even immersive VR environments.

Technological advancements also impact the tools that UX designers use. Tools for prototyping, user testing, and design collaboration are continually evolving, becoming more sophisticated and intuitive. This leads to more efficient design processes and enables the creation of more complex, user-friendly designs.

Technological Influence on Project Management

On the project management front, technology's influence has been equally transformative. Project management tools and platforms have made it possible to manage complex projects more effectively, providing features like task tracking, time logging, resource allocation, and risk management.

The advent of cloud-based project management tools has fostered real-time collaboration and made it easier to manage distributed teams. This has been a significant boon in an era where remote work has become the norm rather than the exception. The ability to easily share files, communicate in real-time, and maintain an overview of project progress from anywhere in the world has transformed the landscape of project management.

The Intersection: Technology's Impact on Managing UX Projects

Now, let's consider the unique intersection of UX design and project management. Managing UX projects involves a delicate balancing act between creative design processes and structured project management principles. Technology has played a crucial role in facilitating this balance.

Take, for instance, design collaboration platforms. These tools combine features of UX design tools and project management software, allowing designers to create and iterate on designs while project managers track progress, manage tasks, and facilitate communication.

Similarly, user testing platforms have revolutionized the way user research is integrated into UX projects. They've made it easier to conduct remote user testing, collate user feedback, and integrate findings into the design process, all within the confines of the project timeline.

However, the intersection of technology, UX design, and project management isn't without its challenges. The rapid pace of technological change can create a sense of perpetual catch-up, as teams have to continuously adapt to new tools, platforms, and design mediums. Furthermore, the integration of complex technologies like AI and AR into UX projects requires specialized skills and a more interdisciplinary approach to project management.

Despite these challenges, the overall impact of technology on UX design and project management is overwhelmingly positive. It has driven the evolution of more user-centric designs, facilitated more efficient project management processes, and opened up new avenues for innovation.

preparing for the future: skills, tools, and mindset

In our previous chapter, we examined the transformative impact of technology on both UX design and project management. Now, we embark on the crucial task of exploring how you, as professionals, can best prepare for the future in these evolving fields. This chapter focuses on the key skills you'll need, the tools you might leverage, and the mindset that will drive your success.

Sharpening Your Skillset

With the pace of technology's evolution, it's vital to keep your skills current and in sync with emerging trends. Here are a few of the essential skills you'll want to hone for the future of UX design and project management:

* Technical proficiency: You don't necessarily need to become a programmer, but a fundamental understanding of the technologies that drive your product or

service will significantly enhance your efficacy as a UX designer or project manager.

* Data analysis: The ability to derive insights from data is a game-changer. With more sophisticated tools gathering user data, the capacity to interpret this information is invaluable for making informed design decisions and managing projects effectively.

* Collaborative capability: As work becomes increasingly remote and distributed, the ability to collaborate effectively across distances is essential. This includes understanding how to leverage collaboration tools and develop strategies for fostering teamwork in virtual environments.

Leveraging Future-Proof Tools

Keeping an eye on the evolving tool landscape is equally important. Here are some tools worth getting comfortable with:

* Design and Prototyping Tools: Stay up-to-date with the latest UX design and prototyping tools like Figma, Sketch, and Adobe XD. These tools are continually evolving and offering new functionalities to create sophisticated designs and interactive prototypes.

* Project Management Platforms: Tools like Jira, Trello, and Asana have become staples in project management. They're continuously improving with integrations for various aspects of project management - resource allocation, risk management, and more.

* Collaboration Tools: Tools like Slack, Microsoft Teams, or Miro can be crucial for effective remote collaboration. Learn how to leverage their features to facilitate communication, share ideas, and foster team cohesion.

* User Testing Platforms: User testing tools such as Usertesting.com or Lookback.io are invaluable for gathering user insights in real-time and can be crucial in informing design decisions.

Adopting the Right Mindset

Beyond skills and tools, the mindset with which you approach your work is critical. Here are a few mindset attributes that can prepare you for the future:

* Adaptive Learning: Embrace a growth mindset. Be open to learning, unlearning, and relearning as technology and trends evolve. Your ability to adapt and learn will be a significant determinant of your success.

* Holistic Thinking: Develop a big-picture perspective. Consider the overall user experience and project goals when making design or management decisions. This allows you to align your actions with strategic objectives.

* User-Centricity: Always place the user at the center of your design decisions. User-centricity is an enduring principle in UX design and should continue to guide your work, irrespective of technological changes.

* Embrace Uncertainty: The future is inherently uncertain, especially in fields heavily influenced by technological advances. Learn to be comfortable with uncertainty and to make decisions even when you don't have all the answers.

As we venture further into the future, we can undoubtedly expect more changes, challenges, and opportunities in the fields of UX design and project management. However, with the right skills, tools, and mindset, you'll be well-prepared to navigate this dynamic landscape.

appendix a: glossary of key terms

By now, you've journeyed through a considerable amount of content spanning the landscape of UX design and project management. We've been immersed in many terms and concepts, some perhaps already familiar, and others, not so much. So, let's dedicate this chapter to a glossary of those key terms that have colored our discussion. We hope that this glossary will serve as a quick reference guide for you as you continue your journey in UX design and project management.

Agile: Agile is a project management and product development approach that champions flexibility, collaboration, and customer value. It encourages adaptive planning, evolutionary development, early delivery, and continual improvement.

Artifact: In Scrum, an artifact is a tangible by-product produced during the development process. Artifacts are typically documents related to project management or product development, such as a product backlog or sprint backlog.

Backlog: A backlog is a list of tasks or features that need to be addressed but aren't a priority in the current development cycle. Backlogs are often divided into product backlogs (broader scope) and sprint backlogs (specific to a particular sprint).

Collaboration Tools: These are software applications designed to help teams work together more effectively. They can facilitate communication, task assignment, document sharing, and more.

Data Analysis: This is the process of evaluating data using analytical and statistical tools to discover useful information and aid in decision making. In the context of UX, data analysis often refers to interpreting user data to guide design decisions.

Figma, Sketch, and Adobe XD: These are popular digital design and prototyping tools used by UX designers. They allow designers to create, test, and iterate on design concepts efficiently.

Holistic Thinking: This refers to understanding and addressing systems as whole entities and not merely the sum of their individual parts. In UX design and project management, this often means considering the entire user experience or project goal when making decisions.

Jira, Trello, Asana: These are widely used project management tools that offer functionalities like task tracking, resource allocation, project timelines, and more.

Prototype: In UX design, a prototype is a mock-up or demo of a product that showcases the functionality, design, and user flow. Prototypes can range from low-fidelity sketches to high-fidelity, interactive models.

Scrum: Scrum is an Agile framework for managing projects. It emphasizes teamwork, accountability, and iterative progress towards a well-defined goal. Scrum involves specific roles, events, and artifacts.

Sprint: In Scrum, a sprint is a set period during which specific tasks or goals must be completed and ready for review. Sprints are typically one to four weeks long.

Stakeholders: Stakeholders are individuals or groups who have an interest in the project's success. They can be internal (team members, managers) or external (clients, users).

User-Centricity: This is an approach to design that involves an in-depth understanding of user behaviors, needs, and motivations. The aim is to create products that align closely with users' needs and provide a seamless user experience.

UX Design: User Experience (UX) design is the process of creating products that provide meaningful and relevant experiences to users. It involves the design of the entire process of acquiring, integrating, and troubleshooting the product.

User Testing: This is a method used in the design process to evaluate a product by testing it with representative users. It provides direct input on how real users use the system.

appendix b: recommended reading and resources

Throughout our discussions on UX design and project management, we've navigated through a sea of concepts, methodologies, and practical applications. But, as with any worthwhile expedition, the journey doesn't have to end here. In this final chapter, we're passing the torch to you, offering a collection of recommended readings and resources that can fuel your continuous learning and growth in these fields.

Books

1. "The Lean Startup" by Eric Ries: If there's a classic book about modern entrepreneurship and product development, this is it. While not specifically about UX or Scrum, its principles are fundamental to understanding how agile teams operate.

2. "Sprint: How to Solve Big Problems and Test New Ideas in Just Five Days" by Jake Knapp, John Zeratsky,

and Braden Kowitz: From Google Ventures, the "Sprint" book is an excellent resource for understanding the rapid prototyping and user testing process.

3. "User Story Mapping: Discover the Whole Story, Build the Right Product" by Jeff Patton and Peter Economy: A fantastic deep dive into user story mapping, a key technique in both UX design and Scrum.

4. "Project Management: A Systems Approach to Planning, Scheduling, and Controlling" by Harold Kerzner: A comprehensive guide to the principles of project management, this book will serve you well in your career.

Online Courses

1. Coursera – Interaction Design Specialization: Created by the University of California San Diego, this series of courses gives a great introduction to UX design principles and practices.

2. Scrum.org – Professional Scrum Master Training: Scrum.org offers multiple levels of training and certification for Scrum, from the basics up to advanced topics.

Websites and Blogs

1. Nielsen Norman Group: This consulting firm publishes a wealth of free articles and reports about various aspects of UX, based on their extensive research.

2. Scrum Alliance: As one of the leading Scrum organizations, Scrum Alliance offers a variety of articles, webinars, and other resources related to Scrum.

3. ProjectManagement.com: A comprehensive resource for project managers, with a wealth of articles, templates, and discussions on a wide range of topics.

Podcasts

1. UX Podcast: A twice-monthly podcast covering a variety of UX topics.

2. Agile for Humans: A podcast focused on the people side of agile, with discussions on everything from team dynamics to best practices for Scrum Masters.

Tools

1. Jira: A project management tool designed specifically for Agile teams.

2. Sketch/Figma/Adobe XD: Popular UX design and prototyping tools.

3. Slack: A team collaboration tool that can help facilitate communication in distributed Agile teams.

Finally, if you're hungry for even more knowledge, don't forget about the power of networking. Consider joining a local UX or project management group, where you can learn from your peers' experiences and share your own insights. And always remember, the pursuit of knowledge is a journey, not a destination. As you continue on your path, you're bound to discover countless resources that resonate with you, fuel your passion, and guide you towards your personal and professional goals.

With this, we turn the final page of our exploration into UX design and project management. But remember, this isn't an end. It's simply the start of the next exciting chapter in your career journey. Good luck, and never stop learning!

appendix c: templates and checklists for ux design and project management

This section aims to provide you with some templates and checklists that can come in handy in your daily work. They serve as practical tools to help you implement the theoretical knowledge we've discussed.

Templates

1. User Persona Template: User personas are critical in UX design, as they allow you to understand and empathize with your users. A good user persona template should include demographics, behavior patterns, motivations, and goals. It should be brief, yet descriptive enough to guide your design decisions.

2. User Story Template: A user story is a short, simple description of a feature told from the perspective of the person who desires the new capability, usually a user or customer of the system. They typi-

cally follow a simple template: "As a [type of user], I want [an action] so that [a benefit/a value]".

3. Product Backlog Template: This is essentially a list of all tasks that need to be done within the project. It should include features, bug fixes, technical work, and knowledge acquisition, with a brief description and an estimate of effort required for each item.

4. Sprint Backlog Template: The sprint backlog is a list of tasks identified by the Scrum team to be completed during the Scrum sprint. It is derived from the product backlog, but contains only those pieces of work that the team anticipates being able to complete in the upcoming sprint.

Checklists

1. UX Design Checklist:

* *Understanding the User:* Have you defined your user personas? Have you conducted user interviews and surveys to gather information about your users?

* *Design:* Have you sketched out your ideas? Have you created wireframes, prototypes, and high-fidelity designs?

* *User Testing:* Have you planned and conducted usability tests? Have you iterated on your designs based on the feedback received?

* *Implementation:* Have you worked closely with developers during the implementation phase? Have

you conducted a final review of the product to ensure it aligns with the designs?

2. Project Management Checklist:

* *Initiating:* Have you identified the project's purpose and scope? Have you gathered a team and defined their roles and responsibilities?

* *Planning:* Have you created a comprehensive project plan, including timeline, budget, and resource allocation? Have you identified potential risks and created a risk management plan?

* *Executing:* Are you managing your team effectively and making sure they have what they need to complete their tasks? Are you communicating regularly with stakeholders and keeping them informed of progress?

* *Monitoring:* Are you tracking progress against your plan? Are you adapting your plan as needed and dealing with any issues that arise?

* *Closing:* Have you reviewed the project's successes and challenges? Have you documented lessons learned for future projects?

Remember, these templates and checklists are merely starting points. The real magic happens when you adapt and personalize these tools to fit your unique work context and team dynamics.

As you turn your attention to the practicalities of UX design and project management, remember that the knowledge you've gained from this book is like a compass, guiding you through the complex landscape of these disciplines. It's an exciting journey, and while there will be challenges, the rewards of creating meaningful, user-focused solutions are well worth the effort. Here's to your success on this incredible journey!